I hope this book becomes your trusted companion as you embark on your journey to mastering Microsoft OneDrive. Whether you're looking to organize your files more efficiently, collaborate seamlessly with others, or achieve new levels of productivity, this guide is here to help you every step of the way.

Think of it as more than just a guide—it's a tool to simplify your life, both personally and professionally. No matter where you are, you have the potential to accomplish great things, and with OneDrive, the possibilities are endless.

This book is written with you in mind. Take your time, explore, and let the tips and step-by-step instructions empower you to succeed with confidence. You've got this, and I'm cheering you on every step of the way!

Table of Content

Introduction to Microsoft OneDrive

What is OneDrive?

OneDrive is a **cloud storage service** developed by Microsoft that allows you to store, sync, and share files securely across devices. It enables you to upload photos, videos, documents, and other types of data, making them accessible from any device connected to the internet, whether it's a computer, tablet, or smartphone.

As part of the Microsoft ecosystem, OneDrive integrates seamlessly with **Microsoft Office** (Word, Excel, PowerPoint, etc.) and other Microsoft products, enhancing the way you manage and access your files. OneDrive offers various plans, including a free plan with limited storage and paid options for additional space and features.

Key Benefits of Using OneDrive

OneDrive is more than just a cloud storage service; it provides several key benefits that make it a valuable tool for individuals and businesses alike:

- **Accessibility Anywhere**: As long as you have an internet connection, you can access your files from any device. This is perfect for people who are always on the go and need their documents on-demand.
- **File Synchronization**: OneDrive allows for automatic synchronization of your files across multiple devices. If you edit a document on your PC, the changes are instantly reflected across all other devices where you've installed OneDrive (including mobile phones and tablets).
- **Secure Storage**: OneDrive uses encryption to protect your files both during transfer and while stored in the cloud. Files are stored with a high level of security to ensure that only you and those you've granted access to can view and edit them.
- **Real-Time Collaboration**: With OneDrive, you can collaborate on files with others in real time. If you're working on a Word document or an Excel sheet, multiple people can make changes simultaneously, and the document is automatically updated.
- **Cost-Effective**: OneDrive offers a free plan with 5 GB of storage, which is more than enough for everyday users. For those who need additional storage, paid plans are affordable, especially when bundled with Microsoft 365 (formerly Office 365), which includes additional features like extra storage, premium apps, and more.
- **Integration with Microsoft Products**: OneDrive works flawlessly with Microsoft Office apps like Word, Excel, PowerPoint, and Outlook, allowing for easy file storage, sharing, and editing directly within the apps.

Overview of OneDrive's Features and Services

OneDrive offers a wide range of features that cater to different user needs, from personal storage to enterprise-level solutions:

- **File Storage and Access**: You can store almost any type of file (documents, pictures, videos, music, etc.). Files stored in OneDrive are organized into folders, which can be accessed easily via the web app, desktop app, or mobile app.
- **File Sharing and Collaboration**: Share files and folders with others, either by sending links or granting direct access to specific users. You can set permissions, such as "view only" or "edit," and collaborate with others using **Office Online** to work together on documents in real-time.
- **File Versioning**: OneDrive keeps a history of changes made to documents. You can easily restore previous versions if needed, making it easy to recover from mistakes or retrieve an earlier version of a document.
- **Syncing Files Across Devices**: OneDrive syncs your files across all devices connected to your OneDrive account, ensuring that you have the latest version of your files no matter which device you're using. This is useful for people who work from different devices or switch between home and work computers.
- **Offline Access**: You can access your files offline by syncing them to your device. This feature allows you to continue working even if you lose internet connectivity. Once you're back online, any changes will sync automatically.
- **OneDrive Personal Vault**: OneDrive offers a secure area called **Personal Vault**, where you can store your most sensitive files. This section requires additional security, such

as facial recognition, fingerprint, or a PIN to access, ensuring that your important documents are extra safe.

- **Integration with Microsoft 365**: For Microsoft 365 subscribers, OneDrive offers 1 TB (terabyte) of storage, and it integrates with tools like **Teams, SharePoint, and Outlook** to streamline workflow and improve collaboration in the cloud.

Understanding Cloud Storage and How OneDrive Fits In

Cloud storage refers to storing data on remote servers that can be accessed over the internet, rather than on physical hard drives or local storage. This means that your files are stored on powerful servers, often managed by a cloud storage provider like **Microsoft**, **Google**, or **Apple**, and are available anytime you need them.

OneDrive is a cloud storage service provided by Microsoft, which means that all the data you upload to OneDrive is stored on **Microsoft's cloud servers**. This is beneficial because:

- **Access Anywhere**: You can access your files from any device with an internet connection, and your data is not tied to a single device. If you lose or damage your computer, your files remain safe in the cloud.
- **Automatic Backups**: With OneDrive, your files are automatically backed up as soon as you upload them, which means you don't have to worry about losing important data due to hardware failures or accidents.

- **Data Redundancy and Reliability**: Cloud storage services like OneDrive are designed to ensure data is stored redundantly across multiple servers, so even if one server fails, your data remains safe and accessible.

OneDrive vs Other Cloud Storage Solutions

While OneDrive is one of the most popular cloud storage services, it's not the only option available. Let's compare OneDrive with other top cloud storage services to understand how it stacks up:

- **OneDrive vs Google Drive**:
  - **Google Drive** offers 15 GB of free storage, which is slightly more than OneDrive's 5 GB free plan. However, OneDrive's deep integration with Microsoft Office applications gives it an advantage for users who rely heavily on Word, Excel, and PowerPoint.
  - Google Drive also integrates well with Google's suite of apps (Docs, Sheets, and Slides), but for Office users, OneDrive provides a more seamless experience.
- **OneDrive vs Dropbox**:
  - **Dropbox** offers cloud storage primarily focused on simplicity and file sharing, with powerful collaboration features. However, OneDrive's pricing and larger storage options (especially when bundled with Microsoft 365) make it a more cost-effective choice for users who need a large amount of storage and integration with Microsoft apps.
  - Dropbox is known for its **third-party app integrations**, but OneDrive offers extensive integration with Microsoft's ecosystem, which is a major advantage for Windows and Office users.
- **OneDrive vs iCloud**:
  - **iCloud** is Apple's cloud storage service, and it is best for users deeply embedded in the Apple ecosystem. OneDrive, on the other hand, is cross-platform,

working on Windows, macOS, iOS, Android, and the web.

- o iCloud's storage plans start at 50 GB, and it integrates well with Apple's applications, but OneDrive's larger free storage and integration with Microsoft Office make it a more versatile option for users who want to work across different platforms.

Chapter 1: Getting Started with OneDrive

Setting Up OneDrive

Creating a Microsoft Account

Before you can start using OneDrive, you need to create a Microsoft account. This account is essential because it allows you to access all Microsoft services, including OneDrive, Outlook, and Office apps.

Step-by-Step Guide to Creating a Microsoft Account:

1. **Go to the Microsoft Sign-Up Page**: Open your web browser and go to the Microsoft account sign-up page at https://signup.live.com/

2. **Enter Your Email Address**: You can use an existing email address (like Gmail or Yahoo) or create a new Outlook or Hotmail address.
3. **Create a Password**: Choose a strong password that contains a mix of uppercase and lowercase letters, numbers, and special characters for security.
4. **Enter Your Name**: Provide your first and last name.
5. **Set Up Additional Security**: You'll be prompted to add a phone number and recovery email address. These are used in case you forget your password or need to verify your identity.
6. **Agree to Terms**: Read through Microsoft's privacy policy and terms of use, then agree to them to complete the sign-up process.
7. **Verify Your Email**: You may be asked to verify your email address by entering a code sent to your inbox.

Once you've successfully created your Microsoft account, you're ready to start using OneDrive!

Signing Up for OneDrive

With a Microsoft account, you're automatically signed up for OneDrive. Your account includes **5 GB of free storage**, which is perfect for personal files like photos, documents, and videos. If you want more space or additional features, you can upgrade to a paid plan later.

Steps to Access OneDrive:

1. **Log In to OneDrive**: Go to the OneDrive website at https://onedrive.live.com/and sign in using your newly created Microsoft account.

2. **Access Your OneDrive**: After logging in, you'll be taken directly to your OneDrive dashboard, where you can start uploading, organizing, and sharing files.

Choosing a OneDrive Plan: Free vs. Paid

OneDrive offers both free and paid plans, with the free plan being an excellent option for casual users and the paid options providing more storage and premium features.

Free Plan (5 GB):

- **5 GB of storage** is included for free with a Microsoft account.
- Perfect for basic file storage and sharing needs, such as keeping documents, photos, and videos.

Paid Plans:

1. **OneDrive Standalone Plan (100 GB)**:
   - Includes **100 GB of storage**.
   - Ideal for individuals who need more space but don't need the full Microsoft 365 suite.
2. **Microsoft 365 Subscription**:

- Includes **1 TB (1,000 GB)** of storage on OneDrive, plus access to Office apps like Word, Excel, PowerPoint, and Outlook.
- Includes **advanced sharing options**, **real-time collaboration**, and **Personal Vault** for extra security.

How to Upgrade:

1. Sign in to your OneDrive account.
2. Go to the **Settings** section (click on the gear icon in the top right).
3. Choose **Upgrade** or **Get OneDrive Premium** and follow the prompts to select the plan that fits your needs.

Installing OneDrive on Windows, Mac, and Mobile Devices

OneDrive is available on various devices, making it easy to access and manage your files wherever you are. Here's how to install OneDrive on different platforms:

On Windows:

1. **Windows 10 and 11** come with OneDrive pre-installed, so you don't need to download it separately.
2. To set it up, click on the **OneDrive** icon in the **system tray** (bottom-right corner).
3. **Sign in** with your Microsoft account.
4. Follow the prompts to choose which folders you'd like to sync to your PC.

On Mac:

1. Download OneDrive from the Mac App Store.
2. Open the app and sign in with your Microsoft account.
3. Select the folders you want to sync to your Mac.
4. The OneDrive icon will appear in the **menu bar**, allowing you to quickly access your files.

On Mobile Devices:

1. **Android**: Download the OneDrive app from the Google Play Store.
2. **iOS**: Download the OneDrive app from the App Store.
3. After installation, open the app and sign in with your Microsoft account.

4. You can upload files, view and share documents, and even scan documents directly using the mobile app.

Syncing Files Across Devices: Once OneDrive is installed on all your devices, your files will automatically sync across them. You can access the latest version of your files whether you're working on your laptop, phone, or tablet.

Navigating the OneDrive Interface

Dashboard Overview

Once you've successfully set up OneDrive, you'll be taken to the **OneDrive Dashboard**. This is your central hub where all your files, folders, and settings are managed. Here's a quick breakdown of the interface:

- **Navigation Bar**: On the left, you'll find the navigation menu, where you can access different sections like **Files**, **Recent**, **Shared**, and **Recycle Bin**.
- **File Area**: This is the main section of the screen where your files and folders are displayed. You can drag and drop files into this area to upload them to OneDrive.

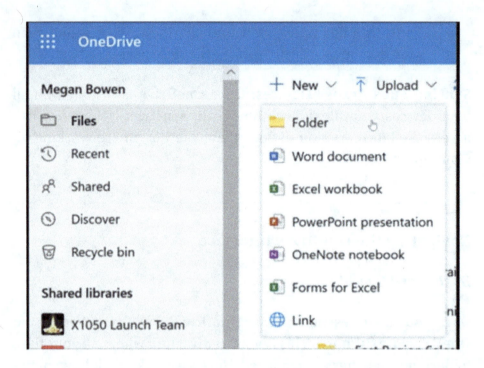

- **Top Toolbar**: Located at the top of the screen, the toolbar provides access to options like **New Folder**, **Upload**, **Download**, **Share**, and **Settings**.

Key Features in the Sidebar

The **sidebar** on the left side of the screen helps you navigate OneDrive quickly and efficiently. Key sections in the sidebar include:

1. **Files**: This is where you'll find all your files and folders stored in OneDrive.
2. **Recent**: View the files you've recently opened or edited.
3. **Shared**: A list of files and folders that others have shared with you, or that you've shared with others.

4. **Personal Vault**: Your extra-secure area for storing sensitive documents. You'll need additional authentication (like a fingerprint or PIN) to access this area.
5. **Recycle Bin**: Deleted files are temporarily stored here before they are permanently erased. You can recover accidentally deleted files from this section.

Understanding File and Folder Organization

OneDrive uses a **folder-based structure** to help you organize your files. You can create folders for different projects or categories, making it easier to find your files when you need them.

Steps to Organize Files:

1. **Create Folders**:
   - Click on **New Folder** in the toolbar or right-click on the screen and select **New Folder**.
   - Name the folder based on its contents (e.g., "Work Documents," "Photos," "Projects").
2. **Move Files Between Folders**:
   - Drag and drop files into different folders for better organization.
   - You can also right-click on a file and select **Move to** to relocate it to another folder.
3. **Renaming Files and Folders**:
   - Right-click the file or folder and select **Rename** to give it a more descriptive name.
4. **Sorting Files**:
   - You can sort your files by name, date modified, or file type by clicking on the column headers.

Customizing OneDrive Settings

OneDrive allows you to customize several settings to better suit your needs. Here's how you can adjust your preferences:

1. **Access Settings**:
   - Click on the **gear icon** in the top-right corner of the dashboard.
   - Select **Settings** from the dropdown menu.
2. **General Settings**:
   - You can set preferences for notifications, language, and theme (light or dark mode).
3. **Sync Settings**:
   - Choose which folders to sync with your device.
   - If you have limited storage, you can select only specific folders to sync to save space.
4. **Storage Management**:
   - View how much space you've used and manage your storage plan.
   - If you're nearing your storage limit, you can delete files, move files to other storage services, or upgrade your OneDrive plan.

Chapter 2: Managing Files and Folders

Uploading Files and Folders to OneDrive

OneDrive makes it easy to upload your files and folders, whether you're on a desktop, mobile device, or using the web. Here's how you can upload files and organize them in the cloud.

How to Upload Files via the Web App

Uploading files via the web app is quick and simple. Whether you're using OneDrive on a computer or tablet, you can upload files directly from your browser.

Step-by-Step Guide:

1. **Log In to OneDrive**: Open your preferred browser and go to onedrive.live.com. Sign in with your Microsoft account.
2. **Navigate to the Folder**: Once logged in, navigate to the folder where you want to upload your files, or create a new folder by clicking the **New Folder** button at the top.
3. **Upload Files**:
   - Click the **Upload** button at the top of the screen.
   - Select **Files** if you want to upload individual files or **Folder** if you want to upload a complete folder.

You can add files to OneDrive in many different ways and then get to them from anywhere.

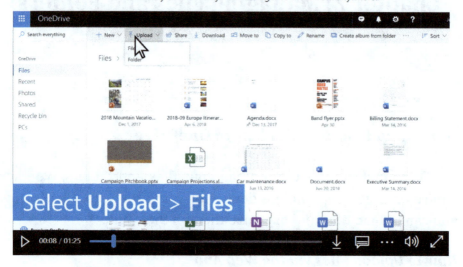

- o Browse your computer for the files/folders you want to upload and select them.

You can add files to OneDrive in many different ways and then get to them from anywhere.

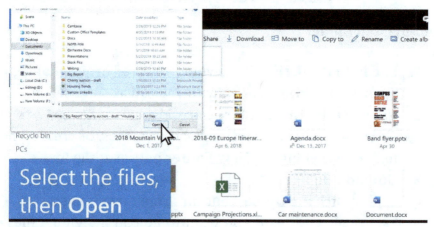

- o Alternatively, you can **drag and drop** files directly from your file explorer into the web app window.

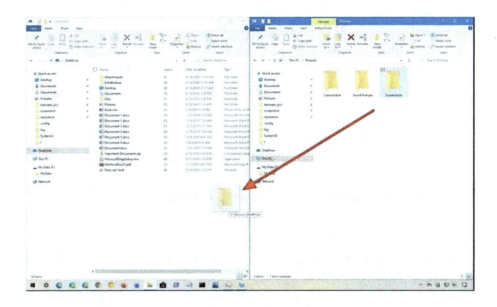

4. **Wait for the Upload to Complete**: A progress bar will appear, showing the status of your upload. Once it's finished, your files will be available in OneDrive.

Using the OneDrive Desktop App for Uploads

The OneDrive desktop app provides seamless integration with your computer's file system, making it easy to manage files and folders between your PC and OneDrive.

Step-by-Step Guide:

1. **Open the OneDrive Folder**: If you have the OneDrive desktop app installed, open the **OneDrive folder** on your computer. You'll find it in the file explorer.
2. **Drag and Drop**: Simply drag and drop the files or folders you want to upload into the OneDrive folder.

3. **Automatic Sync**: The desktop app will automatically sync the files you dropped into the OneDrive folder. This means the files will be uploaded to your OneDrive cloud storage and be available on all devices connected to the same OneDrive account.
4. **Access Your Files**: Once uploaded, your files will appear in your OneDrive web app or mobile app.

Mobile Uploads: How to Add Files on Your Smartphone

OneDrive's mobile app allows you to upload files directly from your smartphone or tablet. Whether you're using Android or iOS, the process is the same.

Step-by-Step Guide for Android and iOS:

1. **Download and Open the App**:
   o Go to the **Google Play Store** or **Apple App Store**, search for OneDrive, and download the app.
   o Open the OneDrive app and sign in with your Microsoft account.
2. **Navigate to the Desired Folder**:
   o Once logged in, navigate to the folder where you'd like to upload the files.
3. **Upload Files**:
   o Tap the **+** (plus) icon at the bottom center of the app.
   o Choose **Upload** from the menu.
   o Select whether you want to upload photos, documents, or files from your phone's gallery or file manager.

- Select the files or photos you want to upload, then tap **Done** to start the upload.
4. **Syncing Files**: Your files will automatically sync to the cloud, making them accessible from any device.

 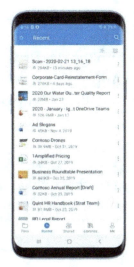 

Batch Uploads and Handling Multiple Files

Uploading multiple files or folders is just as easy as uploading a single file. Whether you're using the web app, desktop app, or mobile app, OneDrive handles batch uploads efficiently.

Step-by-Step Guide for Batch Uploads:

1. **Using the Web App**:
   - Select multiple files or folders by holding down the **Ctrl** (Windows) or **Command** (Mac) key and clicking on each file/folder.

- Drag and drop the selected items into the OneDrive window or use the **Upload** button.
2. **Using the Desktop App**:
   - Open the OneDrive folder on your computer.
   - Select multiple files or folders by holding down the **Ctrl** (Windows) or **Command** (Mac) key while selecting items.
   - Drag them into the OneDrive folder to upload.
3. **Using the Mobile App**:
   - When selecting files for upload, tap on the **multiple files** you want to upload in your phone's file manager or gallery.

Once the files are selected, the upload process will start, and OneDrive will upload them in the background.

Organizing Files in OneDrive

OneDrive gives you several tools to organize your files efficiently. Whether you're managing personal documents or work-related projects, the organizational features in OneDrive will help you stay on top of your files.

Creating and Naming Folders

Creating folders in OneDrive is essential for keeping your files organized. You can create folders for different categories, such as work documents, family photos, or projects.

Step-by-Step Guide:

1. **Create a New Folder**:
   - In the web app, click the **New > Folder** button at the top of the page.

You can add files to OneDrive in many different ways and then get to them from anywhere.

   - In the desktop app, right-click within your OneDrive folder and select **New Folder**.
   - In the mobile app, tap the **+** icon and select **Create Folder**.

2. **Name the Folder**:
   - After creating the folder, enter a descriptive name that reflects its contents (e.g., "Work Projects" or "Vacation Photos").

You can add files to OneDrive in many different ways and then get to them from anywhere.

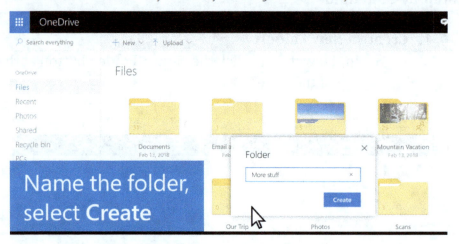

Moving and Copying Files/Folders

OneDrive makes it easy to move or copy files and folders from one location to another.

Step-by-Step Guide for Moving Files:

1. **Move Files in the Web App**:
   - Right-click the file or folder you want to move.
   - Select **Move to** from the context menu.
   - Navigate to the destination folder and click **Move**.
2. **Move Files in the Desktop App**:
   - Simply drag and drop files or folders to the desired location within your OneDrive folder.
3. **Move Files in the Mobile App**:
   - Tap and hold the file or folder you want to move.
   - Select **Move** from the options and choose the destination folder.

Step-by-Step Guide for Copying Files:

- Use the same steps for moving, but instead of selecting **Move to**, choose **Copy to**. This will leave the original file in place while creating a copy in the new location.

Using Tags to Organize Files

While OneDrive doesn't have traditional tags, you can use **descriptive folder names** and **file names** to serve as tags.

For example, instead of creating a separate "work" folder, you can name files in a way that allows you to easily identify their content when you search for them (e.g., "Project_A_Work_Document").

Setting Up a Logical Folder Structure

A clear folder structure is essential for managing large amounts of data. Here's a suggestion for organizing your OneDrive efficiently:

1. **Create Main Categories**:
    - **Personal**: For photos, videos, and personal documents.
    - **Work**: For projects, work-related files, and presentations.
    - **Shared**: For files you share with others or collaborate on.
2. **Use Subfolders**:
    - Within each main category, use subfolders to further organize your files. For example, in the "Work" folder, you can have subfolders like "Reports," "Presentations," and "Budgeting."

3. **Maintain a Consistent Naming Convention**:
   ○ When naming files, use a consistent system to keep everything in order. You could use dates or categories (e.g., "Report_2023_01" or "Family_Vacation_2022").

Searching for Files in OneDrive

OneDrive has a powerful search feature that helps you quickly locate your files, even if you have a large amount of content stored in your account.

Using the Search Bar Efficiently

To search for a file in OneDrive:

1. **Click on the Search Bar**: At the top of the OneDrive window, you'll find a search bar. Click on it.
2. **Enter Keywords**: Type in the file name or keywords related to the file you are searching for. OneDrive will start showing relevant results as you type.
3. **Refine Your Search**: If you have many results, you can refine your search by using specific keywords or the **filters** on the left side of the search results.

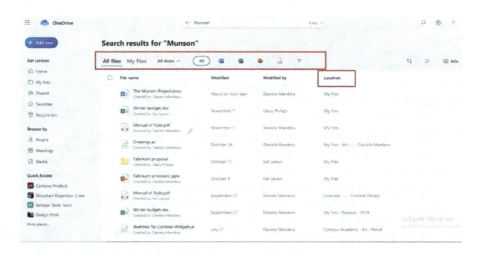

Advanced Search Options and Filters

OneDrive provides several filters to help narrow down your search:

1. **Filter by File Type**: If you know the type of file you're looking for (e.g., Word, Excel, or PDF), you can use the filters to display only files of that type.
2. **Filter by Date**: You can also filter by **date modified** to find recently edited or uploaded files.

3. **Search by Owner or Shared**: If you've shared files or have files shared with you, you can use the filter to narrow down results to only shared items or files owned by others.

Chapter 3: Syncing Files Across Devices

Understanding OneDrive Sync

OneDrive's syncing feature allows you to access your files from any device with an internet connection. Syncing makes sure that the files you edit or upload on one device are updated across all of your devices. This section will explain how syncing works and the features that OneDrive offers to optimize your experience.

What is File Syncing and How It Works

File syncing means that your files are continuously updated across all of your devices. Once you make a change to a file, the updated version will automatically appear on all devices connected to the same OneDrive account.

How Syncing Works:

- **Local and Cloud Copies**: When you upload a file to OneDrive, it is stored in the cloud. If you have OneDrive installed on multiple devices, a local copy of the file is also stored on each device.
- **Two-Way Syncing**: Changes made on one device will sync automatically to the cloud and then to all other connected devices. For example, if you add a new file to your OneDrive

folder on your PC, it will sync to OneDrive in the cloud and then be accessible on your other devices.

- **Background Syncing**: OneDrive syncs your files in the background, ensuring they're up-to-date without you needing to do anything. It syncs automatically as long as you have an internet connection.

Syncing Files to Your PC, Mac, and Mobile Devices

OneDrive can be synced to multiple devices, allowing you to access and manage your files wherever you go. Here's how to sync your files on different devices:

Syncing on a Windows PC:

1. **Install OneDrive**: OneDrive comes pre-installed on Windows 10 and 11. If you don't have it installed, you can download the desktop app from the OneDrive website.
2. **Sign In**: Open the OneDrive app, sign in with your Microsoft account, and choose the folders you want to sync.
3. **Syncing Files**: Once synced, any file you place in the OneDrive folder on your PC will automatically sync to the cloud and be available on other devices.

Syncing on a Mac:

1. **Install OneDrive**: Download the OneDrive app from the Mac App Store.
2. **Sign In**: Launch the OneDrive app, sign in with your Microsoft account, and select the folders to sync.

3. **Syncing Files**: The OneDrive folder will be available in your Finder, and any files you place in it will automatically sync across devices.

Syncing on Mobile Devices (iOS and Android):

1. **Install the OneDrive App**: Download the OneDrive app from the Apple App Store (iOS) or Google Play Store (Android).
2. **Sign In**: Open the app, log in with your Microsoft account, and choose which folders to sync for offline access.
3. **Syncing Files**: Files are synced when you're connected to Wi-Fi or mobile data. You can view and upload new files while connected to the internet. For offline access, you can select specific files to make available offline.

OneDrive Files On-Demand: Save Space on Your Device

OneDrive Files On-Demand is a feature that allows you to view and access all your files in OneDrive without taking up space on your device. Only the files you need are downloaded to your device, while the rest remain in the cloud.

How to Use Files On-Demand:

1. **Enable Files On-Demand**:
   o On **Windows 10/11**, right-click the OneDrive icon in the system tray, go to **Settings**, and make sure the **Files On-Demand** option is checked.
   o On **Mac**, open OneDrive preferences and enable Files On-Demand.
2. **Accessing Files**:

- o Files appear in your OneDrive folder, but they are marked with one of three icons:
    - **Cloud Icon**: The file is stored in the cloud and doesn't take up space on your device. You need an internet connection to access it.
    - **Green Check Icon**: The file is downloaded and available offline.
    - **Blue Sync Icon**: The file is syncing to your device.

3. **Making Files Available Offline**:
    - o Right-click on a file or folder and select **Always keep on this device** to ensure it's available offline.

4. **Freeing Up Space**:
    - o If you're low on space, you can right-click a file or folder and select **Free up space** to remove it from your device while keeping it in OneDrive.

This feature is particularly useful for devices with limited storage, as it allows you to access all your files without cluttering up your device's storage.

Managing Sync Settings

Managing your OneDrive sync settings ensures that you control which files and folders are synced to your devices. By customizing sync settings, you can optimize your storage space, avoid sync errors, and better manage the flow of your files across devices.

Choosing Which Folders to Sync

OneDrive allows you to selectively choose which folders to sync to your devices, which can be particularly helpful if you have limited space or if certain files don't need to be accessed on every device.

Step-by-Step Guide to Choose Folders to Sync:

1. **On Windows or Mac**:
   o Right-click the **OneDrive icon** in the system tray (Windows) or menu bar (Mac).

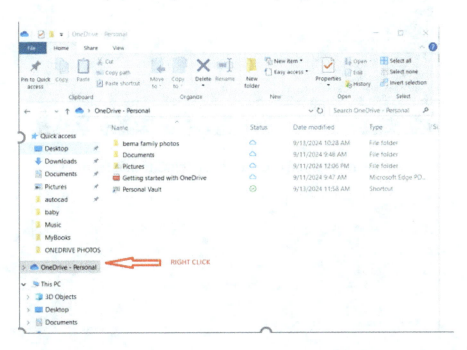

   o Select **Settings** from the dropdown menu.

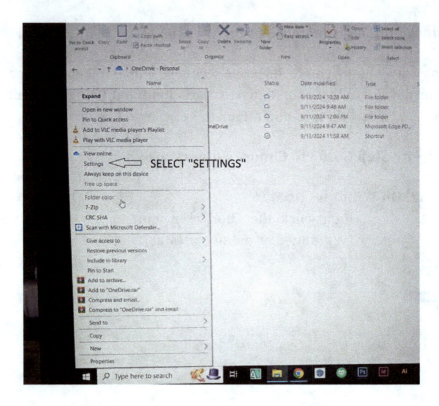

o   Under the **Account** tab, click **Choose folders**.

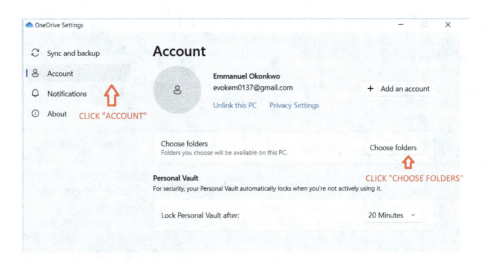

o In the pop-up window, check the boxes next to the folders you want to sync to your device. Uncheck any folders you don't want to sync.

o Click **OK** to confirm your choices.

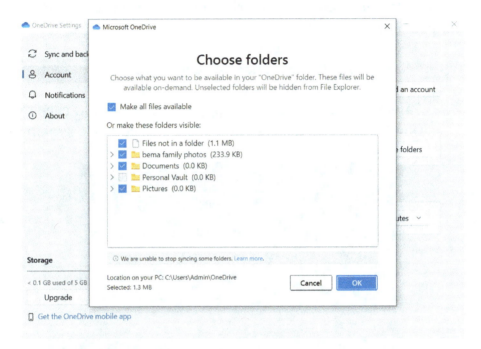

2. **On Mobile**:

o In the OneDrive mobile app, go to the **Settings** section.

o Select **Offline Files** to see which files are available for offline use. You can choose which files or folders to make available offline.

How to Sync OneDrive Files to External Drives

OneDrive is typically designed to sync to your primary drive (usually C: on Windows), but you can change the location of the OneDrive folder to an external drive if you want to save space on your computer.

Step-by-Step Guide for External Drive Syncing:

1. **Pause Syncing**: Before making any changes, right-click the OneDrive icon in the system tray and select **Pause syncing**.

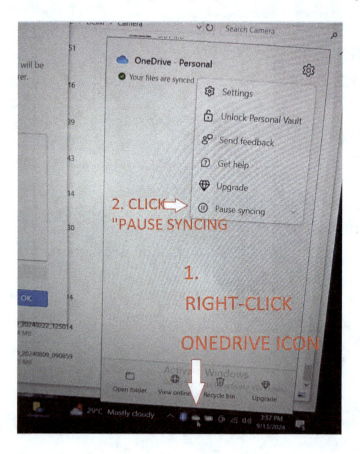

2. **Move the OneDrive Folder**:
    - Open **OneDrive Settings** by right-clicking the OneDrive icon.
    - Under the **Account** tab, click **Unlink this PC** and confirm.
    - Go to the external drive and create a new folder for OneDrive.
    - Reopen OneDrive and sign in. When prompted to choose a location for your OneDrive folder, select the folder on your external drive.
3. **Resume Syncing**: After moving the folder, click **Resume syncing** to start syncing files to your external drive.

Note: OneDrive must remain connected to the external drive in order to sync properly. If the drive is disconnected, syncing will stop.

Resolving Sync Errors: Common Issues and Solutions

Sync errors can sometimes occur, but they are usually easy to resolve. Below are some common issues and how to fix them.

Common Sync Issues:

1. **File Syncing is Stuck**: If OneDrive seems stuck on syncing a file, try restarting the OneDrive app or rebooting your computer.
2. **File or Folder Conflict**: OneDrive may show a sync error if the same file is edited on multiple devices. Resolve this by checking for duplicates and keeping only one version of the file.

3. **Out of Space**: OneDrive may stop syncing if your account reaches its storage limit. To fix this, delete unnecessary files, upgrade your OneDrive plan, or move files to an external drive.
4. **Network Issues**: If syncing is slow or not working, check your internet connection. Ensure you have a stable connection for syncing to work smoothly.
5. **File Type Issues**: OneDrive may not sync certain file types, such as system files or files with unsupported extensions. Ensure your files are supported by OneDrive.

How to Troubleshoot:

- **Check OneDrive Status**: Right-click the OneDrive icon in the system tray or menu bar, and check the status. If there's an error, it will be listed there.
- **Use the OneDrive Troubleshooter**: On Windows, go to **Settings > Update & Security > Troubleshoot**, and select **OneDrive** from the list of troubleshooters.

By managing sync settings effectively, you can keep your OneDrive organized and ensure that your files are always accessible across devices.

Chapter 4: Using OneDrive on Different Platforms

OneDrive on Windows and Mac

OneDrive is designed to integrate seamlessly with both Windows and Mac operating systems. This section will cover setting up OneDrive on these platforms, managing files, and using OneDrive's features effectively.

Setting Up OneDrive on Windows 10 and 11

OneDrive comes pre-installed on Windows 10 and 11, making setup simple. Here's how to get started:

Step-by-Step Guide:

1. **Sign In**:
    - On a fresh Windows installation, OneDrive prompts you to sign in with your Microsoft account during setup. If not prompted, click the **OneDrive icon** in the taskbar or start menu.
2. **Choose Your Folders**:
    - After signing in, you'll be asked to select which folders to sync with OneDrive. You can choose all folders or select specific folders to save space.
3. **Set Up Files On-Demand**:

- o   Make sure **Files On-Demand** is enabled to save storage space. This feature allows you to see and access your OneDrive files without downloading them to your device.
4. **Start Syncing**:
    - o   After setup, your OneDrive folder will appear in **File Explorer** under **Quick Access** and **This PC**. Any files placed in this folder will automatically sync to the cloud.

Using OneDrive with File Explorer on Windows

Once OneDrive is set up on Windows, it integrates with **File Explorer**, making it easy to manage files directly from your PC. Here's how to use it:

1. **Navigate to the OneDrive Folder**:
    - o   Open **File Explorer**, and on the left sidebar, click on **OneDrive** under **Quick Access**. This folder behaves like any other folder, but the files are synced with the cloud.
2. **Managing Files**:
    - o   **Add Files**: Simply drag and drop files into the OneDrive folder.
    - o   **File Status**: Files show different icons to indicate their status:
        - ▪   **Cloud Icon**: Stored in the cloud, available online only.
        - ▪   **Green Checkmark**: Available offline.
        - ▪   **Blue Circular Arrow**: Currently syncing.
3. **File Management**:

- You can organize your OneDrive folder by creating subfolders, renaming files, and moving them just like in any other folder on your computer.

OneDrive on Mac: Setup and Usage

Setting up OneDrive on a Mac is similar to the Windows setup, with some Mac-specific differences:

Step-by-Step Guide:

1. **Download OneDrive**:
   - Go to the **Mac App Store** and download the **OneDrive** app or download it from the **OneDrive website**.
2. **Sign In**:
   - After installation, sign in with your Microsoft account.
3. **Choose Folders to Sync**:
   - Select the folders you wish to sync. You can always change this later.
4. **Complete Setup**:
   - OneDrive will now begin syncing your files. You'll see the OneDrive icon in the top menu bar, which shows sync status and offers options like pausing or resuming sync.

Managing OneDrive Files in Finder on Mac

On Mac, OneDrive integrates with **Finder** to allow you to manage your files directly from your desktop.

1. **Access OneDrive**:
   - In **Finder**, you'll see a folder called **OneDrive** in the left sidebar under **Favorites**. Here you can view and manage all your synced files.
2. **File Status**:
   - Files in **Finder** will show status indicators similar to those on Windows:
     - **Cloud Icon**: File is stored in the cloud and will require an internet connection to open.
     - **Green Checkmark**: The file is available offline and stored on your device.
3. **Adding Files**:
   - To add files to OneDrive, simply drag them into the OneDrive folder in **Finder**. The files will sync automatically with the cloud.
4. **File Organization**:
   - You can organize your OneDrive files into folders, rename files, and move them around within **Finder**, just like in any other directory.

OneDrive on Mobile Devices

OneDrive's mobile apps for iOS and Android bring cloud storage right to your fingertips. You can upload, access, and manage your files directly from your smartphone or tablet.

Installing OneDrive on iOS and Android

To use OneDrive on mobile, you'll first need to download the OneDrive app from your device's app store:

- **For iOS**: Go to the **App Store**, search for **OneDrive**, and tap **Get**.

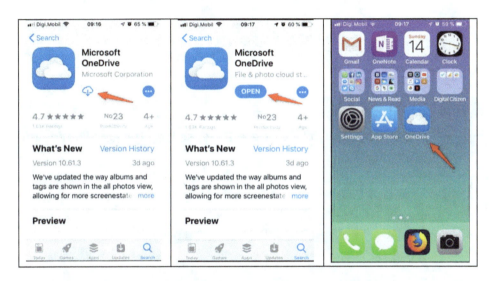

Tap OneDrive. Doing so will open it in the Files app. If you don't see your cloud accounts listed on this page, first tap **Locations** near the top of the page.

You may need to tap the "New Locations" option if you don't see OneDrive listed, and then tap the switch for OneDrive to the "ON"

- **For Android**: Go to **Google Play**, search for **OneDrive**, and tap **Install**.

Once the app is installed, open it and sign in with your Microsoft account to begin using OneDrive on your mobile device.

Uploading and Accessing Files from Your Phone

Uploading files from your mobile device to OneDrive is simple:

1. **Upload Files**:
   - Open the **OneDrive app**.
   - Tap the **plus (+) icon** and choose **Upload**.
   - Select files or photos from your gallery, camera, or other apps.

2. **Access Files**:
   - All files synced to OneDrive are available on your mobile device. Open the app to browse or search for any file.
   - Files you've uploaded or synced will be available for online or offline viewing, depending on your settings.

Using the OneDrive App Features on Mobile

The OneDrive app provides several useful features to make managing your files on mobile easy:

1. **Scan Documents**:
   - You can use the **Scan** feature in the app to digitize physical documents. Simply open the app, tap **Scan**, and capture the document using your phone's camera.
2. **File Sharing**:
   - Share files directly from your phone. Select a file, tap the **Share** icon, and choose how you want to share it (email, link, etc.).
3. **Offline Access**:
   - Make important files available offline by selecting the file and choosing **Make Available Offline**. This allows you to access files even without an internet connection.
4. **Photo Backup**:
   - Use the **Camera Upload** feature to automatically upload photos from your phone's gallery to OneDrive. This feature ensures your photos are backed up securely in the cloud.

OneDrive Web Application

The OneDrive web application allows you to access, upload, and manage files from any browser. This is ideal when you're using a computer without the OneDrive desktop app installed or when you're away from your usual devices.

Accessing OneDrive from Any Browser

To access OneDrive from the web:

1. Open any **browser** (Chrome, Edge, Safari, etc.).
2. Go to the **OneDrive website**: onedrive.com.
3. Sign in with your **Microsoft account**.

Once signed in, you'll be able to view, upload, and manage your files directly from the browser interface.

Uploading, Sharing, and Managing Files Online

You can manage your OneDrive files easily through the web app:

1. **Uploading Files**:
    o Click the **Upload** button at the top of the page.
    o Select the files or folders from your computer that you want to upload to OneDrive.
2. **Sharing Files**:
    o To share a file, right-click on the file and select **Share**.
    o You can choose to share via a **link**, email, or invite others to edit or view the file.

3. **Managing Files**:
   - Create folders to organize files.
   - Rename or delete files by selecting them and clicking **Rename** or **Delete** in the toolbar.
   - Use **Version History** to restore previous versions of a file.

Using OneDrive's Web Interface for Quick Access

The OneDrive web interface is simple to navigate and allows you to manage your files quickly:

1. **Quick Access**:
   - The **Recent** section shows files you've recently opened or edited, providing a fast way to access frequently used documents.
2. **Search**:
   - Use the **Search bar** at the top to find specific files by name or content.
3. **File Previews**:
   - Click on a file to preview it directly in the browser, even if you don't have the appropriate software installed on your device.
4. **Syncing from the Web**:
   - You can also manage syncing by accessing the **OneDrive settings** from the web interface. Adjust which folders are available offline, or initiate syncing to a new device.

Chapter 5: Sharing Files and Folders

Sharing files and folders in OneDrive allows you to collaborate with others, whether for work, school, or personal projects. OneDrive offers several options to help you control how and with whom you share your files. In this chapter, you will learn about the various sharing features, permissions, and collaboration tools available in OneDrive.

How to Share Files and Folders in OneDrive

Sharing files and folders in OneDrive is easy, whether you want to send a file to a colleague, share a document with a friend, or give access to a group project.

Generating Shareable Links

OneDrive makes it simple to generate a shareable link that can be sent to anyone. Here's how to do it:

Step-by-Step Guide:

1. **Select the File or Folder**:
   o Open your **OneDrive** and locate the file or folder you wish to share.
2. **Right-Click and Choose Share**:
   o Right-click on the file/folder and select **Share** from the context menu. Alternatively, click on the file to

highlight it, and then click the **Share** icon in the top menu.

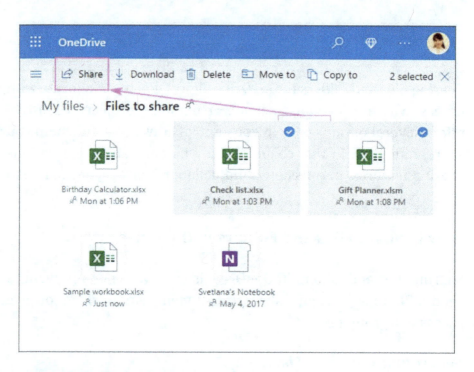

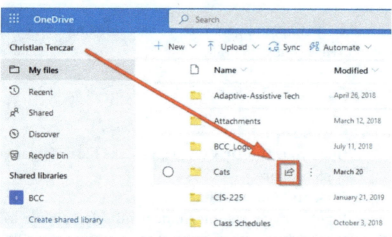

Using the share icon beside the file or folder

3. **Choose Link Settings**:
   o In the Share menu, you'll be given a few link options:
      - **Anyone with the link**: Shareable by anyone with the link, no sign-in required.
      - **People in your organization**: Limit sharing to people within your company or group.
      - **Specific people**: Share only with specific people by entering their email addresses.

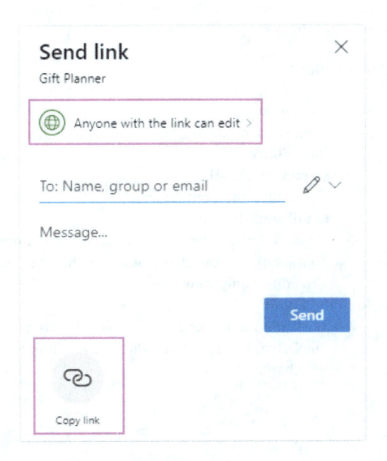

4. **Copy the Link**:
    o   After selecting your sharing preferences, click **Copy Link**. This generates the link, which you can then paste in an email, message, or document.
5. **Send the Link**:
    o   After copying the link, paste it into your email, message, or any other form of communication.

Sending Files via Email

For a more direct approach, you can send a file through email using OneDrive's built-in integration with your email provider.

Step-by-Step Guide:

1. **Select the File to Send**:
    o   Right-click on the file or folder you want to share and click **Share**.
2. **Choose Send via Email**:
    o   Select the **Email** option from the share menu.
3. **Enter Email Details**:
    o   Type in the recipient's email address and a message (optional). You can also choose whether the recipient can edit or only view the file.
4. **Send the Email**:
    o   Click **Send** to email the file directly through OneDrive. The recipient will receive a link to access the shared file.

Setting Permissions: View vs. Edit

When sharing files or folders, OneDrive allows you to set specific permissions on how the recipients interact with your files.

1. **View Only**:
   - If you want the recipient to only view the file without making changes, select the **Can View** option. This is ideal for sharing documents you want to be read but not edited.
2. **Edit**:
   - If you want the recipient to have the ability to modify the file, select the **Can Edit** option. This is useful for collaboration, such as when working on a shared document or project.

Advanced Sharing Options

While basic file sharing in OneDrive is easy and convenient, there are additional advanced options available to further control and secure your files.

Restricting Access with Passwords and Expiration Dates

If you need to add extra security to your shared files, OneDrive allows you to set a password and expiration date for shared links.

Step-by-Step Guide:

1. **Select the File or Folder to Share**:
   o Right-click on the file or folder you want to share and choose **Share**.
2. **Open Link Settings**:
   o In the sharing options menu, click on **Link Settings** (the small gear icon next to the link).

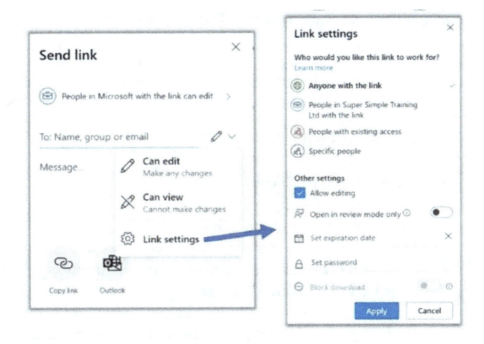

3. **Set a Password**:
   - Enable the **Require Password** option and set a password. The recipients will need this password to access the shared file.
4. **Set an Expiration Date**:
   - Enable **Set an expiration date** and choose when the link should expire. After this date, the file will no longer be accessible via the shared link.
5. **Apply Settings**:
   - Click **Apply**, then generate the shareable link as usual. This ensures that only those with the password can access the file, and they'll only have access until the expiration date.

Sharing Files with People Outside Your Organization

OneDrive allows you to share files with people outside of your organization, such as friends, clients, or collaborators from other businesses.

Step-by-Step Guide:

1. **Select the File to Share**:
   - Right-click on the file and choose **Share**.
2. **Choose "Anyone with the Link"**:
   - If you want people outside your organization to access the file, select **Anyone with the link**.
3. **Enter External Email Addresses**:
   - Enter the email addresses of the external recipients. If your organization permits sharing with people outside the organization, you will be able to send the link to non-company email addresses.
4. **Send the Link**:
   - Choose the appropriate permissions (view or edit) and send the link.

Note: Your organization's admin may set restrictions on sharing outside the organization. If this is the case, you will not see the option to share with external users.

Tracking Who Has Access to Your Shared Files

OneDrive allows you to see who has accessed your shared files and track their activity, which can be helpful for collaboration and security.

Step-by-Step Guide:

1. **Select the File or Folder**:
   o Right-click on the shared file/folder and select **Manage Access**.
2. **View Who Has Access**:
   o Under **Manage Access**, you can see who has access to the file, along with their permissions (view/edit). You can also see the **link settings** that were applied.
3. **View Activity**:
   o Click on **Activity** to view recent actions taken on the file, such as edits, comments, or downloads.
4. **Stop Access**:
   o To revoke someone's access, click on the **X** next to their name or link. This will remove their access to the shared file or folder.

Collaborating with Others Using OneDrive

OneDrive is not just for file storage – it's a powerful tool for collaboration. By using OneDrive's real-time co-authoring, commenting features, and activity tracking, you can work together with others seamlessly.

Real-Time Co-Authoring in Microsoft Office Files

OneDrive allows multiple people to work on a Microsoft Office file simultaneously, with real-time updates.

Step-by-Step Guide:

1. **Open a Document**:
   - Open a Microsoft Office file (Word, Excel, PowerPoint) from your OneDrive.
2. **Invite Collaborators**:
   - Click **Share** to send an invitation to collaborate. You can choose to share with people inside or outside your organization.
3. **Collaborating in Real Time**:
   - Once collaborators open the file, you can see their changes as they make them. Each person's cursor is highlighted, and changes are instantly visible.
4. **Save and Sync Changes**:
   - All changes are automatically saved in real-time to OneDrive, ensuring everyone has the latest version of the document.

Adding Comments and Notes to Documents

Adding comments and notes can help you and your collaborators track feedback or suggestions directly in the document.

Step-by-Step Guide:

1. **Open the Document**:
   - Open your Office file from OneDrive.
2. **Add Comments**:
   - In Word, Excel, or PowerPoint, select the text or cell where you want to leave a comment.

- o   Right-click and choose **New Comment** or click the **Comment** button in the ribbon.

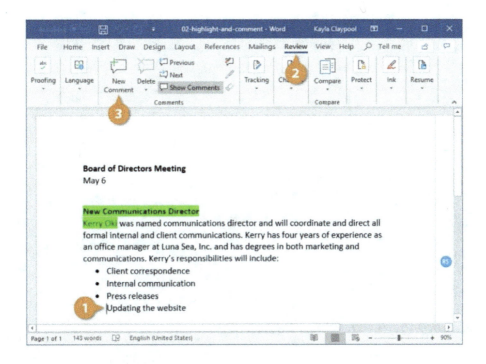

3. **View and Reply to Comments**:
- o   You can reply to existing comments or mark them as resolved once they have been addressed.

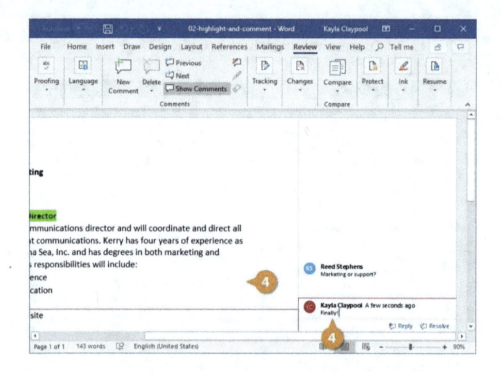

Managing and Viewing File Activity

Tracking file activity allows you to see who's interacting with your shared files and what they're doing.

Step-by-Step Guide:

1. **Open Manage Access**:
   - Right-click on the file or folder and select **Manage Access**.

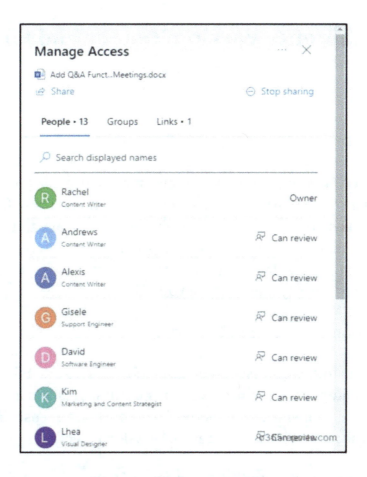

2. **View Activity**:
   - ○ Click on **Activity** to see recent interactions. You'll be able to see who viewed, edited, or commented on the file.
3. **Adjust Permissions if Necessary**:
   - ○ Based on the activity, you may decide to change permissions or revoke access from certain users.

Chapter 6: Version History and File Recovery

OneDrive provides powerful tools for managing your files, including version history and file recovery options. These features help you keep track of changes, restore older versions, and recover files that may have been accidentally deleted or altered. In this chapter, we will explore how to make the most of these features to ensure the integrity and safety of your files.

Understanding Version History

Version history is an essential feature of OneDrive that allows you to view and restore previous versions of files. This is particularly useful for documents that undergo frequent changes, ensuring that you can always go back to a previous version if needed.

Viewing and Restoring Older Versions of Files

OneDrive automatically saves versions of your files, allowing you to go back in time and view or restore an earlier version.

Step-by-Step Guide:

1. **Navigate to the File**:
   o In OneDrive, locate the file for which you want to view the version history.
2. **Right-Click and Select Version History**:

- Right-click on the file, and from the context menu, select **Version History**.

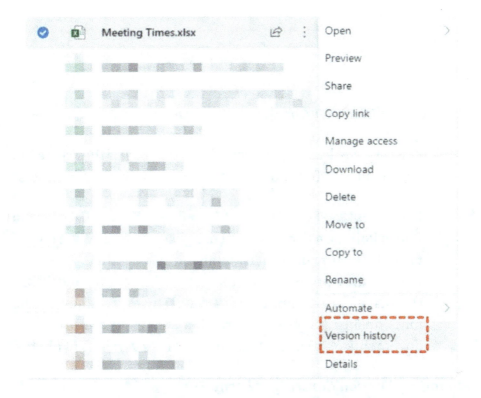

- Alternatively, select the file, click on the ellipsis (...) in the top menu, and choose **Version History**.

3. **View Available Versions**:
   - A list of available versions will appear, showing the date, time, and author of each version.

4. **Restore a Previous Version**:
   - To restore a version, click on the version you want, and you'll have options to either **Restore** it (replacing the current version) or **Open** it for review.

How Version History Works with Documents and Photos

Version history works seamlessly with most types of files stored in OneDrive, including Office documents, photos, and other file types.

- **Documents**: For Office files like Word, Excel, and PowerPoint, OneDrive saves changes automatically. You can view the document's revision history in real time.
- **Photos and Images**: For image files like JPEGs and PNGs, OneDrive also supports version history, though the functionality may be more limited compared to text documents. You can still restore previous versions of photos.

Managing Version Control for Large Files

Managing version history for large files requires attention, as frequent changes to these files can lead to a significant number of versions.

Tips for Managing Large Files:

1. **Delete Older Versions**:
   - If version history accumulates too many versions for large files, you can manually delete old versions to keep your storage usage in check.

2. **Set Versioning Limits**:
   o For more controlled version management, especially for large files, consider adjusting your OneDrive settings (in **Library Settings**) to limit the number of versions retained.

Recovering Deleted Files from OneDrive

Accidental file deletion happens to everyone, but OneDrive makes it easy to recover deleted files from the **Recycle Bin**. Whether you need to restore a single file or an entire folder, OneDrive's recovery tools are user-friendly.

Using the Recycle Bin to Restore Files

When files are deleted from OneDrive, they are moved to the **Recycle Bin**, where they can be restored easily.

Step-by-Step Guide:

1. **Open the OneDrive Recycle Bin**:
   o In the OneDrive web interface, click on **Recycle Bin** in the left-hand sidebar.
2. **Select the Files to Restore**:
   o Browse through the deleted files, select the ones you want to restore by clicking the checkboxes next to them.
3. **Restore the Files**:

- After selecting the files, click on the **Restore** button at the top. The files will be returned to their original location in your OneDrive.

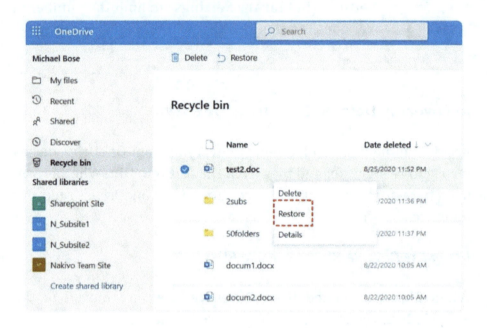

How Long Do Files Stay in the Recycle Bin?

Files in the OneDrive Recycle Bin are kept for **30 days** by default. After 30 days, they are permanently deleted. If you want to keep a file beyond that period, you should restore it within the 30-day window.

- **Files in the Second-Stage Recycle Bin**: If you've already emptied the main Recycle Bin, you may still find your files in the second-stage Recycle Bin. You can restore these files in the same way, but they will be permanently deleted after 93 days.

Restoring Files from the OneDrive Web App vs. Desktop

You can restore files from both the OneDrive web app and the desktop app, although the process may differ slightly.

- **From the Web App**: You can access the Recycle Bin directly through the OneDrive web interface. The web app provides the most detailed recovery options.
- **From the Desktop App**: The OneDrive desktop app does not directly allow access to the Recycle Bin. However, files deleted from the desktop app are synced with the web app's Recycle Bin, so you can restore them via the OneDrive website.

Recovering from Accidental Changes or Deletions

Sometimes, you may make accidental changes to a document or delete a file you didn't intend to. Thankfully, OneDrive offers several ways to undo these changes and recover from mistakes.

Undoing Changes in Office Documents

For documents edited in Microsoft Office (Word, Excel, PowerPoint), OneDrive offers powerful undo features.

Step-by-Step Guide:

1. **Open the Document:**
   o Open the file in the respective Office application (Word, Excel, PowerPoint).

2. **Use the Undo Feature**:
   - ○ In most Office applications, you can press **Ctrl + Z** (or **Command + Z** on Mac) to undo recent changes.
3. **Restore from Version History**:
   - ○ If the undo feature isn't sufficient, you can revert the document to an earlier version by accessing the **Version History** and selecting a previous version.

Recovering Entire Folders or Large File Groups

If you've accidentally deleted a large group of files or an entire folder, you can restore these easily from the Recycle Bin or by using the version history for the folder.

Step-by-Step Guide:

1. **Navigate to the Recycle Bin**:
   - ○ Go to the OneDrive **Recycle Bin** via the web app.
2. **Select Multiple Files or a Folder**:
   - ○ You can select multiple files or a complete folder to restore at once. The process is the same as restoring individual files.
3. **Restore Folder Structure**:
   - ○ When restoring a folder, OneDrive will also restore the folder structure as it was, making sure everything is placed back in its original location.

Chapter 7: Security and Privacy Settings

In today's digital world, securing your files and ensuring your privacy is crucial. OneDrive provides several robust tools to help you protect your data and manage security settings. This chapter will guide you through the steps to safeguard your files, protect shared information, and defend against phishing and malware attacks.

Protecting Your Files with OneDrive

OneDrive offers a variety of features to help protect your files, from managing security settings to ensuring your data is encrypted. By properly configuring these settings, you can ensure your files are safe from unauthorized access and cyber threats.

Managing Security and Privacy Settings

OneDrive offers numerous security settings to help protect your files from unauthorized access and ensure that your private information stays safe.

Step-by-Step Guide:

1. **Access Security Settings**:
    o Go to the OneDrive website, click on the **Gear icon** in the top-right corner, and select **Settings**.

- Under **Security & Privacy**, you'll find options to customize your security preferences.

2. **Managing File Permissions**:
   - For each file or folder, you can set permissions on who has access to your data. To do this, right-click on a file or folder, select **Manage Access**, and choose from options like "Anyone with the link" or "Specific People."

3. **Setting Up Activity Alerts**:
   - To keep track of who is accessing your files, set up alerts that notify you of any activities such as uploads, downloads, or edits.

Enabling Two-Factor Authentication (2FA)

Two-factor authentication (2FA) adds an additional layer of security by requiring a second form of identification (in addition to your password) when logging into OneDrive.

Step-by-Step Guide:

1. **Sign In to Your Microsoft Account**:
   - Visit the Microsoft Account Security page at https://account.microsoft.com/security and sign in.

2. **Enable 2FA**:
   - Under **Security settings**, find the option for **Two-step verification** and click **Set up two-step verification**.

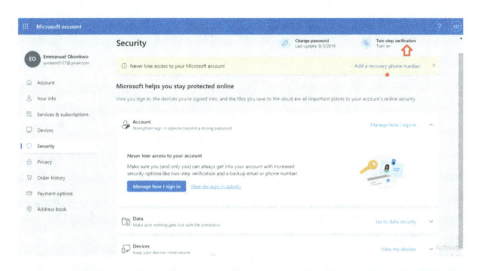

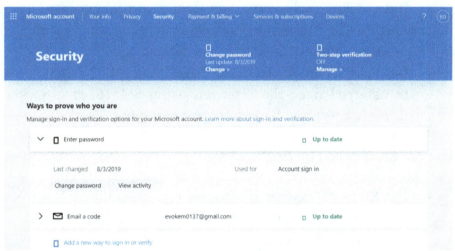

o You'll be prompted to choose a secondary method of authentication (SMS, phone call, or authenticator app).

3. **Verify Setup**:

o Once the setup is complete, you'll receive a verification code sent to your secondary method

(SMS, email, or app). Enter this code to finalize 2FA activation.

4. **Test the Feature**:
   o Log out of your OneDrive account and sign back in to make sure that the second authentication step works as expected.

Understanding Encryption and File Protection

OneDrive uses encryption to protect your files, ensuring they are safe both during upload and while stored on their servers.

- **Data at Rest**: Files stored on OneDrive are encrypted using AES 256-bit encryption, ensuring that your data is protected even when not being actively accessed.
- **Data in Transit**: Files are also encrypted when being transferred over the internet, using SSL (Secure Sockets Layer) encryption to prevent interception.

Tips for Enhanced File Protection:

- **Use Strong Passwords**: Ensure that your Microsoft account has a strong, unique password to minimize the risk of unauthorized access.
- **Encrypt Sensitive Files**: For highly sensitive files, consider adding additional layers of encryption using third-party tools before uploading them to OneDrive.

Securing Shared Files and Folders

When you share files or folders in OneDrive, it's important to control who has access and what actions they can take. OneDrive provides several features to help you secure your shared files, including restricted access and expiration dates for links.

Restricting Access to Sensitive Information

If you need to share sensitive information, you can restrict access to ensure that only the right people can view or edit your files.

Step-by-Step Guide:

1. **Right-Click on the File or Folder**:
   - Navigate to the file or folder you want to share, then right-click and select **Share**.
2. **Set Permissions**:
   - In the share menu, you can choose who can access the file. Select either:
     - **Anyone with the link**: Open access (not recommended for sensitive files).
     - **People in your organization**: Restricts access to your organization.
     - **Specific people**: You can specify exactly who can access the file.
3. **Set View or Edit Permissions**:
   - Choose whether users can **Edit** or only **View** the file. For more sensitive files, it's advisable to set the permission to **View** only.

Using Expiration Dates and Passwords for File Links

OneDrive offers the ability to secure shared files by setting expiration dates for links or adding passwords for additional protection.

Step-by-Step Guide:

1. **Generate a Link**:
   o After selecting the file or folder to share, click on **Copy link**.
2. **Set Expiration Date**:
   o Choose the **Expiration date** option to set how long the link will remain active.
3. **Set a Password**:
   o You can also require a password to open the shared file. This is especially useful for sensitive files that you want to protect with an extra layer of security.

Monitoring Who Views and Edits Your Files

To ensure that your files are being accessed and edited by the right people, you can monitor their activity in OneDrive.

Step-by-Step Guide:

1. **Check File Activity**:
   o Right-click on the file and select **Details**. Here, you'll be able to view the activity history, including who has viewed or edited the file.
2. **Track Edits and Comments**:

- For files being collaborated on, you can see real-time changes, comments, and suggestions that others have made.

3. **Use Version History**:
   - In addition to monitoring activity, the **Version History** feature allows you to keep track of changes made to the file over time.

How to Protect Against Phishing and Malware

Phishing and malware attacks are some of the most common cybersecurity threats. OneDrive includes several security features to help protect you from such attacks.

Recognizing Suspicious Links and Emails

Phishing attacks often involve fraudulent emails or messages that try to trick you into sharing sensitive information. Be aware of the following signs:

- **Unusual Email Addresses**: Look out for email addresses that don't match the official Microsoft domain.
- **Suspicious Links**: Hover over links to check where they lead. Avoid clicking on links that don't look legitimate or that point to unfamiliar websites.

Tips for Avoiding Phishing:

- **Never Share Your Credentials**: Don't provide your Microsoft password or account details via email or on suspicious websites.
- **Use Multi-Factor Authentication**: As discussed earlier, enable 2FA to protect your account from unauthorized access.

Setting Up Security Alerts in OneDrive

OneDrive lets you set up security alerts to notify you of suspicious activities, such as unusual login attempts or changes made to shared files.

Step-by-Step Guide:

1. **Access Security Settings**:
   - Go to your Microsoft account's **Security & Privacy** settings.
2. **Enable Activity Alerts**:
   - Scroll down to the **Security alerts** section and toggle on notifications for activities like logins from unfamiliar locations or devices.
3. **Monitor Security Alerts**:
   - You'll receive email alerts or notifications on your device whenever a security-related event occurs in your OneDrive account.

Chapter 8: Backup and Restore

OneDrive isn't just a place to store your files—it's also an essential tool for backing up and restoring data. With its easy-to-use features, OneDrive can become your primary backup solution, ensuring your important files are safe and recoverable when needed. This chapter will guide you through the process of using OneDrive to back up your files, restore them when necessary, and explore advanced backup options for more control over your data.

Backing Up Files with OneDrive

Using OneDrive as your backup solution ensures that your files are protected in case of device failure or accidental deletion. OneDrive can automatically back up certain folders, such as your Documents, Pictures, and Desktop folders, and it also allows you to manually back up specific files and folders.

Using OneDrive as Your Primary Backup Solution

OneDrive can become your go-to tool for file backup, ensuring that your important documents, photos, and other files are securely stored in the cloud. It's particularly useful for maintaining access to your files from multiple devices.

Step-by-Step Guide:

1. **Enable OneDrive Backup:**

- o Open the **OneDrive app** on your PC.
- o Right-click the **OneDrive icon** in the taskbar and select **Settings**.
- o Under the **Backup** tab, click **Manage backup**.

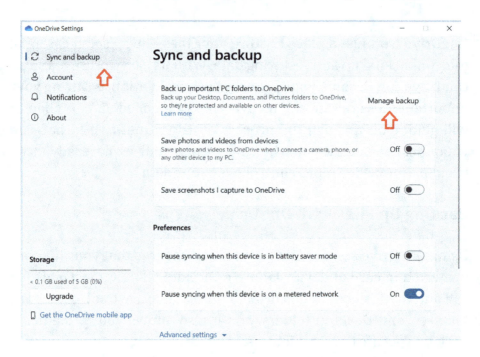

- o Select the folders you want to back up to OneDrive, such as **Desktop**, **Documents**, and **Pictures**.

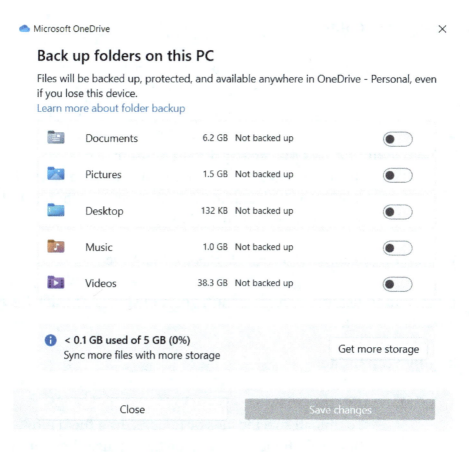

2. **Backup Other Files**:

    ○ You can also drag and drop files or folders into the OneDrive folder on your device. These will automatically sync to the cloud.

Setting Up Automatic Backups for Documents and Photos

OneDrive can automatically back up your important files like documents and photos, reducing the need for manual backups.

Step-by-Step Guide:

1. **Automatic Backup for Documents and Pictures**:
   - On Windows, you can use OneDrive to automatically back up your **Documents** and **Pictures** folders. This is done by syncing them to the OneDrive cloud.
2. **Backup Photos Automatically on Mobile**:
   - On mobile devices, enable **Camera Upload** in the OneDrive app to automatically back up photos and videos taken with your phone.

Backing Up Specific Folders and Files to OneDrive

In addition to default folder backups, you can choose specific files or folders to back up.

Step-by-Step Guide:

1. **Manually Upload Files**:
   - To upload specific files or folders, drag them into the OneDrive folder on your device or use the **Upload** button in the OneDrive web app.
2. **Organize Your Files**:
   - Create a logical structure within OneDrive to categorize your backup files. For example, you might create folders for **Work**, **Family Photos**, and **Personal Documents**.

Restoring Files and Folders

Accidents happen. Files can be deleted, changed, or lost. Thankfully, OneDrive provides several methods for restoring files or folders, whether it's retrieving files from the Recycle Bin or recovering previous versions of a document.

Steps for File Recovery via OneDrive

OneDrive's file recovery system allows you to restore lost or deleted files with ease.

Step-by-Step Guide:

1. **Access the OneDrive Web App**:
   o Go to OneDrive.com and log in to your account.
2. **Open the Recycle Bin**:
   o On the left sidebar, click **Recycle bin** to view all deleted files.
3. **Restore Files**:
   o Select the files or folders you want to restore and click **Restore** to recover them to their original location.

How to Restore Files from the Recycle Bin

OneDrive's Recycle Bin stores deleted files for up to 30 days, giving you ample time to recover them if necessary.

Step-by-Step Guide:

1. **Navigate to the Recycle Bin**:

- o From the OneDrive web interface, click **Recycle bin** in the sidebar.
2. **Select Files for Restoration**:
   - o Select the deleted files you want to restore and click **Restore** to return them to their original location.

Recovering Files from Previous Versions

OneDrive also keeps older versions of documents, allowing you to revert to previous versions if necessary. This feature is especially useful for restoring earlier drafts or undoing unwanted changes.

Step-by-Step Guide:

1. **Right-Click the File in OneDrive**:
   - o On your PC or via the OneDrive web app, right-click the file you want to restore.
2. **Select Version History**:
   - o Choose **Version history** to view a list of previous versions.
3. **Restore the Desired Version**:
   - o Select the version you want to restore and click **Restore** to recover it.

Advanced Backup Options

For those who need more control over their backups, OneDrive offers advanced options like folder backup and integration with File History on Windows. These options can give you an even higher level of security and peace of mind for your files.

Setting Up Folder Backup on Your PC

OneDrive allows you to back up specific folders on your PC, ensuring that all important data is continuously synced to the cloud.

Step-by-Step Guide:

1. **Access OneDrive Settings**:
   - Right-click the OneDrive icon in the taskbar and select **Settings**.
2. **Manage Folder Backup**:
   - Under the **Backup** tab, click **Manage backup**. Select the folders (Desktop, Documents, Pictures) that you want to back up to OneDrive.
   - Once set up, these folders will automatically sync with OneDrive.

Using OneDrive with File History on Windows

File History is a feature built into Windows that automatically backs up files on your PC. You can use it in conjunction with OneDrive to create an even more robust backup solution.

Step-by-Step Guide:

1. **Enable File History**:
   - Go to **Settings > Update & Security > Backup**.
   - Click **Add a drive** and select your OneDrive folder as the backup location.
2. **Set Up Backup Frequency**:
   - Customize how often you want File History to back up your files and how long to keep previous versions.

Chapter 9: Advanced OneDrive Features

In this chapter, we will explore some of the more advanced features of OneDrive that enhance collaboration, integration with Microsoft Office and Teams, and offline access to your files. These tools allow you to take full advantage of OneDrive's capabilities, increasing your productivity and efficiency, whether you are working online or offline.

Using OneDrive with Microsoft Office

OneDrive's integration with Microsoft Office makes it incredibly easy to access, edit, and collaborate on Office files. Whether you're working on documents, spreadsheets, or presentations, OneDrive ensures seamless access and storage for your files.

Accessing and Editing Office Files in OneDrive

OneDrive allows you to open and edit Microsoft Office files directly within the cloud. This feature ensures that your documents are always up-to-date and easily accessible from any device.

Step-by-Step Guide:

1. **Accessing Office Files:**
    - Log in to **OneDrive** via the web or open the **OneDrive app** on your device.

- o Navigate to the folder containing your Office files (e.g., Word, Excel, or PowerPoint).
- o Click on the file you wish to open. It will launch in **Microsoft Office Online** for quick editing.

2. **Editing Files**:
   - o After opening the file, you can edit it directly within the Office Online interface. Changes are automatically saved to OneDrive as you make them, eliminating the need to manually save your progress.

Saving Documents Directly to OneDrive from Word, Excel, and PowerPoint

You can also save documents, spreadsheets, and presentations directly to OneDrive from the Microsoft Office desktop apps. This ensures your files are automatically backed up in the cloud and accessible from anywhere.

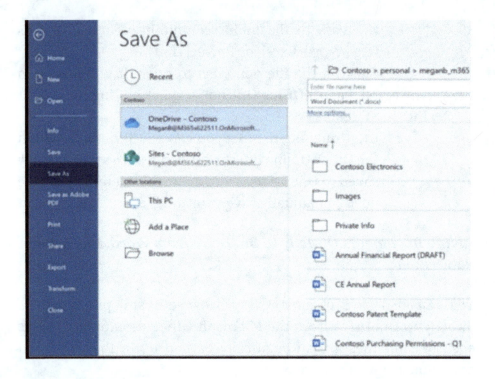

Step-by-Step Guide:

1. **Save a New Document to OneDrive**:
   - In any Microsoft Office app (Word, Excel, or PowerPoint), go to **File > Save As**.
   - Select **OneDrive** as the location to save your document. You can choose your preferred OneDrive folder to organize your files.
2. **Save Existing Documents to OneDrive**:
   - Open your document and go to **File > Save As > OneDrive** to move the document to the cloud if it's not already saved there.

Collaboration Features for Office 365 Users

If you're using Office 365, OneDrive offers enhanced collaboration features. Multiple users can work on the same file simultaneously, making real-time collaboration smooth and efficient.

Step-by-Step Guide:

1. **Share the Document**:
   o Open the document you wish to collaborate on and click **Share** in the upper right corner.
   o Choose whether to invite people by email or generate a shareable link.
2. **Collaborate in Real-Time**:
   o Once shared, collaborators can edit the document at the same time. You will see their changes in real-time, and you can also leave comments or track changes.

Using OneDrive with Microsoft Teams

Microsoft Teams is an essential collaboration tool for businesses and organizations, and OneDrive integrates seamlessly with it. Files stored in OneDrive can be shared directly in Teams, making it easy to collaborate and stay organized.

Integrating OneDrive with Teams for Collaboration

By linking OneDrive with Microsoft Teams, you can access and share your files more efficiently during team collaborations.

Step-by-Step Guide:

1. **Link OneDrive to Teams**:
   - Open **Microsoft Teams** and go to the team channel where you want to share a file.
   - Click on the **Files** tab at the top of the channel and select **OneDrive** to view your cloud storage.
   - Choose the file or folder you want to share and click **Share** to post it in the channel.

Uploading and Sharing Files in Teams Channels

OneDrive makes it easy to upload and share files directly within Teams, ensuring that all team members have access to the same documents and information.

Step-by-Step Guide:

1. **Upload Files to Teams**:
   - In the Teams channel, go to the **Files** tab and click **Upload**.
   - Select the files you want to upload from your local drive or **OneDrive**.
2. **Share Files in Teams Chats**:
   - In a private chat, click the **Attach** icon (paperclip) and select **OneDrive** to choose a file from your cloud storage.
   - You can also directly link to OneDrive files in Teams by selecting **Copy Link** and pasting it into a chat.

Co-authoring Documents in Real-Time During Meetings

One of the standout features of Teams and OneDrive integration is the ability to co-author documents in real time while in a Teams meeting. This enables seamless collaboration during virtual meetings.

Step-by-Step Guide:

1. **Open the Document in Teams**:
   - During a meeting, share a document by clicking **Share Content > Share File**.
   - Open the document directly from OneDrive or upload it if it's not already shared.
2. **Collaborate in Real-Time**:
   - Once the document is shared, all meeting participants can edit it simultaneously, seeing updates instantly.

Offline Access to OneDrive Files

OneDrive's offline access feature allows you to continue working on your files even when you don't have an internet connection. This is particularly useful for mobile workers or when you're in an area with poor connectivity.

How to Use Files Offline in OneDrive

To work offline, you must first ensure that your files are available offline on your device.

Step-by-Step Guide:

1. **Enable Offline Files on Desktop**:
   - ○ Right-click the OneDrive icon in the taskbar and click **Settings**.
   - ○ Under the **Account** tab, click **Choose folders** to select the folders you want to be available offline.
2. **Enable Offline Files on Mobile**:
   - ○ Open the **OneDrive app** on your mobile device.
   - ○ Find the file or folder you want to access offline, tap the three dots beside it, and select **Make Available Offline**.

Syncing Files for Offline Access

Once offline access is enabled, OneDrive will sync your selected files and make them available for use without an internet connection.

Step-by-Step Guide:

1. **Automatic Syncing**:
   - ○ When you enable offline access, OneDrive will automatically sync the selected files to your device.
   - ○ Any changes you make offline will sync with OneDrive once you're back online.

Managing Offline Files on Mobile Devices

On mobile devices, managing offline files is just as important for ensuring productivity while away from the internet.

Step-by-Step Guide:

1. **View and Manage Offline Files**:
   - Open the **OneDrive app** and tap on **Offline** to view all your offline files.
   - To free up space, tap the three dots beside a file and select **Remove from Offline**.

Chapter 10: Troubleshooting OneDrive

In this chapter, we will guide you through common issues users encounter with OneDrive and provide solutions to fix them. Troubleshooting can sometimes be a daunting task, but with the right approach, most issues can be resolved quickly and easily. Whether you're dealing with syncing problems, login issues, or platform-specific errors, this chapter will help you get your OneDrive running smoothly again.

Common OneDrive Issues and How to Fix Them

Many users face common issues with OneDrive, including syncing problems, login errors, and storage space limits. Understanding how to troubleshoot these issues can save you time and effort.

Syncing Problems and How to Resolve Them

Syncing issues are one of the most frequent problems with OneDrive. These issues can arise when files don't sync across devices, or when changes made to files are not reflected on OneDrive or other devices.

Step-by-Step Guide:

1. **Check Your Internet Connection**:

o   Ensure you have a stable internet connection. A slow or intermittent connection can prevent files from syncing properly.

2. **Check the OneDrive Status**:
   o   Visit the **OneDrive status page** to ensure there are no ongoing service outages affecting syncing.

3. **Restart OneDrive**:
   o   Right-click the **OneDrive icon** in the taskbar and select **Close OneDrive**.
   o   Then, reopen the OneDrive app to restart syncing.

4. **Check Syncing Folders**:
   o   Make sure the files you want to sync are located in OneDrive folders. Non-synced files won't sync automatically unless placed within the OneDrive folder.

5. **Clear Cache**:
   o   Clear the cache for the OneDrive app to resolve issues related to corrupted sync data.

OneDrive Login Issues and Fixes

Sometimes, users encounter issues logging into OneDrive, whether it's due to incorrect credentials, account issues, or service interruptions. Here's how to troubleshoot login problems:

Step-by-Step Guide:

1. **Check Your Credentials**:
   o   Ensure you are using the correct email address and password linked to your OneDrive account.

2. **Reset Your Password**:

- o If you've forgotten your password, visit the **OneDrive password recovery page** to reset it.
3. **Sign Out and Back In**:
   - o Sign out of OneDrive and sign back in with the correct account credentials.
4. **Check for Account Restrictions**:
   - o Ensure your account is not locked or suspended due to violations or security concerns. Visit the **Microsoft Account Security Page** for help.
5. **Clear OneDrive Credentials**:
   - o Go to **Control Panel > Credential Manager**, and remove any stored OneDrive login credentials. Then try logging in again.

Storage Space Limit Reached: What to Do

OneDrive has a storage limit, and when it's reached, you won't be able to upload new files until you free up space or increase your storage limit.

Step-by-Step Guide:

1. **Check Your Current Storage**:
   - o Open OneDrive, and check how much space you've used and how much is available by clicking on the **Storage** tab in the settings menu.
2. **Free Up Space**:
   - o Delete unnecessary files or move them to an external drive to free up space in your OneDrive account.
3. **Upgrade Storage**:

- o If you need more space, you can upgrade your OneDrive storage plan by going to **Microsoft 365's subscription page** or purchasing additional storage through your Microsoft account.

File Not Syncing? Troubleshooting Sync Conflicts

When multiple devices or users are editing a file, sync conflicts can arise. These conflicts prevent your files from syncing correctly across all devices.

Identifying Sync Errors and Resolving Them

Sync errors often appear as red or yellow icons next to files in OneDrive. Identifying the root cause of the error is the first step in resolving it.

Step-by-Step Guide:

1. **Look for Sync Error Icons**:
   - o Red X or yellow warning icons next to files indicate a sync issue. Hover over the icon to see the error message.
2. **Resolve the Error**:
   - o Follow the error message instructions to resolve it, such as renaming a file, checking for a corrupt file, or ensuring your device has enough space to complete the sync.

How to Handle Syncing Conflicts with Multiple Devices

Syncing conflicts are more common when files are accessed or edited from multiple devices simultaneously. When this happens, OneDrive may create duplicates or fail to sync changes properly.

Step-by-Step Guide:

1. **Identify Duplicate Files**:
   - OneDrive often adds "(conflicted copy)" to the file name when it creates a duplicate due to syncing conflicts.
2. **Resolve Conflicts**:
   - Review each version of the conflicting file and decide which version you want to keep. Delete the duplicates or save the most recent version to avoid confusion.

Fixing Sync Issues on Mobile Devices

Syncing on mobile devices (iOS and Android) can be tricky due to intermittent internet connections, app settings, or device-specific issues. Here's how to troubleshoot common sync issues on mobile devices:

Step-by-Step Guide:

1. **Ensure OneDrive App is Updated**:
   - Go to your device's app store and check for any available updates for the **OneDrive app**. Updating the app often resolves syncing issues.
2. **Check Background App Refresh**:

- o On iOS, ensure **Background App Refresh** is enabled for OneDrive in **Settings > General > Background App Refresh**.
- o On Android, ensure that **Battery Optimization** doesn't restrict OneDrive's background activity.
3. **Check Mobile Data Settings**:
    - o Ensure OneDrive is allowed to use mobile data for syncing when you're not connected to Wi-Fi.

Troubleshooting OneDrive on Windows, Mac, and Mobile

Different platforms may present unique OneDrive challenges, but with these troubleshooting steps, you can quickly fix most issues.

Fixing Common Problems on Different Platforms

Whether you're using OneDrive on **Windows**, **Mac**, or **Mobile**, specific issues can crop up on each platform. Here's how to address them:

Step-by-Step Guide:

1. **Windows**:
    - o If OneDrive is not syncing, check your internet connection and restart the OneDrive app.
    - o Ensure that OneDrive is up to date through the **Windows Store** or **Settings**.
2. **Mac**:
    - o Ensure that **macOS** is up to date, as older versions may cause syncing issues.

- o Restart OneDrive via the **Finder** or **Activity Monitor** if it freezes.
3. **Mobile Devices**:
   - o Make sure your **mobile OS** is updated and that the OneDrive app is allowed to run in the background.

Dealing with OneDrive Crashes or Freezes

Sometimes, OneDrive may crash or freeze on your computer or mobile device. This can usually be resolved by restarting the app or the device.

Step-by-Step Guide:

1. **Restart OneDrive**:
   - o Close the OneDrive app, reopen it, and check if the issue is resolved.
2. **Clear Cache or Reinstall**:
   - o On Windows, clear the OneDrive cache by going to **Settings > Apps > OneDrive > Advanced Options**.
   - o On mobile devices, uninstall the app and reinstall it to resolve any corrupted app data.

Uninstalling and Reinstalling OneDrive

If OneDrive continues to malfunction, reinstalling the app might fix persistent issues.

Step-by-Step Guide:

1. **Uninstall OneDrive**:

- On **Windows**, go to **Settings > Apps > OneDrive > Uninstall**.
- On **Mac**, open **Finder**, go to the **Applications** folder, and drag OneDrive to the trash.

2. **Reinstall OneDrive**:
   - After uninstalling, download the latest version of OneDrive from the **Microsoft website** or app store and reinstall it.

Chapter11: OneDrive for Business

OneDrive for Business is an enterprise-grade solution designed for organizations that need more robust file storage, sharing, and collaboration tools. It is built to meet the needs of businesses while maintaining the ease-of-use that OneDrive users are familiar with. In this chapter, we'll provide an overview of OneDrive for Business, compare it with personal OneDrive accounts, and delve into its advanced features for managing files in a corporate setting.

Overview of OneDrive for Business

OneDrive for Business is designed to help companies manage files, enhance collaboration, and ensure security in the workplace. It builds on the same core functionality as OneDrive but adds enterprise-level features like deeper integration with Microsoft tools and advanced admin controls.

Differences Between OneDrive Personal and OneDrive for Business

While both OneDrive Personal and OneDrive for Business offer cloud storage, they cater to different needs. Here are the key differences:

1. **Target Audience**:

- OneDrive Personal is designed for individual users and personal file storage.
- OneDrive for Business is designed for organizations to store, share, and collaborate on work files securely.

2. **Storage Capacity**:
   - **OneDrive Personal** typically offers 5 GB of free storage, with the option to purchase more via OneDrive subscriptions.
   - **OneDrive for Business** usually comes with a larger storage capacity (1 TB per user, with options to increase storage for businesses with larger needs).

3. **Collaboration Tools**:
   - **OneDrive for Business** integrates more deeply with enterprise tools like **SharePoint** and **Microsoft Teams**, enabling seamless collaboration within the organization. OneDrive Personal does not offer these integrations.

4. **Security and Compliance**:
   - **OneDrive for Business** offers advanced security features, including compliance with industry standards such as GDPR and HIPAA. Personal accounts are more limited in this respect.

5. **Admin Control**:
   - **OneDrive for Business** offers a range of administrative controls to manage user permissions, data access, and security. Personal accounts lack these administrative capabilities.

Integrating OneDrive with SharePoint and Microsoft Teams

OneDrive for Business works seamlessly with **SharePoint** and **Microsoft Teams**, which are essential tools for collaboration in a business environment.

1. **Integration with SharePoint**:
   - OneDrive for Business stores files that are linked to SharePoint sites. Users can sync files between SharePoint and OneDrive for easy access, ensuring that all documents are in sync across the team.
   - SharePoint serves as a central repository for document management, while OneDrive for Business acts as an individual's personal file storage solution that can be easily shared and collaborated on.
2. **Integration with Microsoft Teams**:
   - Microsoft Teams is a hub for team collaboration, and OneDrive for Business integrates directly with Teams to store files. Documents shared in Teams are automatically saved to the associated user's OneDrive for Business account.
   - Teams users can collaborate on documents in real time, and any changes made to shared documents are reflected instantly across all users' OneDrive accounts.

Using OneDrive for Business in the Enterprise Setting

In the enterprise setting, OneDrive for Business serves as a vital component of an organization's document management and collaboration system. It allows for secure file storage, sharing, and collaboration across teams and departments, whether employees are working in the office or remotely.

1. **Remote Work**:
   - OneDrive for Business supports remote work by allowing employees to securely access and collaborate on files from anywhere with an internet connection.
2. **Advanced Search Features**:
   - OneDrive for Business offers powerful search capabilities that allow users to quickly locate documents and files stored across both OneDrive and SharePoint, improving efficiency in the workplace.
3. **Multi-device Access**:
   - OneDrive for Business can be accessed from multiple devices, including desktops, laptops, tablets, and smartphones, enabling users to stay productive no matter where they are.

Managing OneDrive for Business

Managing OneDrive for Business involves configuring permissions, security settings, and collaboration features to ensure the smooth operation of your business's file-sharing system. Administrators have access to a variety of management tools that allow them to oversee the organization's OneDrive environment.

Admin Features and File Permissions

One of the most powerful features of OneDrive for Business is the ability for admins to manage permissions and access to files. Admins have full control over user accounts, file access, and storage.

1. **User Management**:
   - Admins can create, delete, and manage user accounts within OneDrive for Business. This ensures that only authorized personnel can access specific files and folders.
2. **File Permissions**:
   - Admins can set granular permissions for files and folders, determining whether users can view, edit, or share files. These permissions can be customized for each employee or team, ensuring that sensitive information is only accessible to authorized individuals.
3. **External Sharing Control**:
   - Admins can control whether or not files and folders can be shared externally with people outside the organization. This provides an added layer of security when dealing with sensitive business information.

Sharing and Collaboration in a Business Environment

OneDrive for Business makes it easy for teams to share and collaborate on documents in a secure and controlled environment.

1. **Real-Time Collaboration**:

- OneDrive for Business supports **co-authoring**, allowing multiple users to work on the same document at the same time. Changes are automatically saved, and users can see each other's edits in real time.

2. **File Sharing**:
   - Users can share files with others inside and outside the organization. When sharing externally, admins can set permissions and even require a password or expiration date for additional security.

3. **Version History**:
   - OneDrive for Business automatically saves versions of documents, enabling teams to track changes and restore previous versions if necessary.

Security and Compliance Features in OneDrive for Business

Security and compliance are critical in a business environment, and OneDrive for Business includes robust tools to help meet organizational and legal requirements.

1. **Data Loss Prevention (DLP)**:
   - OneDrive for Business includes **DLP** capabilities that help detect and prevent the accidental sharing of sensitive information, such as credit card numbers, Social Security numbers, or company secrets.

2. **Encryption**:
   - Files stored in OneDrive for Business are encrypted both at rest and in transit, ensuring that your data is always protected.

3. **Compliance with Legal and Regulatory Standards**:

- OneDrive for Business is designed to comply with a variety of industry regulations, including GDPR, HIPAA, and SOC 2, ensuring that your company meets the necessary legal requirements for data protection.

4. **Audit Logs**:
   - Admins can track who is accessing files, what actions they are taking, and whether any unusual behavior is occurring. This is especially important for maintaining compliance and identifying potential security risks.

5. **Retention and Archiving**:
   - Admins can configure retention policies to automatically archive or delete files after a certain period, helping the organization stay compliant with legal and regulatory requirements.

Appendices

Glossary of Terms

In this glossary, we define key terms related to OneDrive and cloud storage. These terms will help you understand the essential concepts and features when using OneDrive.

1. **Cloud Storage**: A system where data is stored on remote servers accessed via the internet, instead of on a local hard drive or physical device.
2. **Syncing**: The process of ensuring that the same data (files or folders) is accessible across all your devices connected to OneDrive. Syncing updates files in real-time, ensuring consistency across platforms.
3. **OneDrive**: A cloud storage service from Microsoft that allows users to store files online, access them remotely, and share them across multiple devices.
4. **File Explorer**: A tool in Windows that allows users to navigate and manage files and folders on their computer. OneDrive can be accessed and managed from File Explorer in Windows.
5. **SharePoint**: A web-based collaboration platform used in businesses for managing documents and information sharing, often integrated with OneDrive for Business.

6. **Co-Authoring**: The ability for multiple users to edit the same document simultaneously, often used in OneDrive with Microsoft Office files.
7. **Version History**: A feature in OneDrive that tracks the changes made to files and allows you to restore previous versions of documents or files.
8. **Recycle Bin**: A storage area in OneDrive that temporarily holds deleted files before they are permanently removed. You can restore files from the Recycle Bin within a specified time frame.
9. **Two-Factor Authentication (2FA)**: A security process that requires two forms of identification before granting access to an account. It adds an extra layer of protection for OneDrive users.
10. **Encryption**: The process of converting data into a secure format that prevents unauthorized access, ensuring that files stored in OneDrive are protected.

Quick Reference Guide

Here is a quick reference guide with key shortcuts and tips to help you use OneDrive efficiently:

Key Shortcuts:

- **Ctrl + N**: Create a new document or folder in OneDrive.
- **Ctrl + C / Ctrl + V**: Copy and paste files or folders.
- **Ctrl + Z**: Undo an action, such as moving or deleting a file.

- **Shift + Delete**: Permanently delete a file or folder without sending it to the Recycle Bin.
- **Ctrl + Shift + E**: Open the OneDrive web app.
- **Ctrl + F**: Open the search bar to find files or folders in OneDrive.
- **Alt + D**: Open the address bar in File Explorer to quickly navigate to a folder or file.

Tips for Efficient OneDrive Use:

1. **Enable Automatic Sync**: Ensure that OneDrive is set to automatically sync your files for easy access from any device.
2. **Organize Your Files**: Use folders and subfolders to keep your files organized. This makes it easier to find and manage documents.
3. **Use Tags and Descriptions**: Add tags or descriptions to files for better searchability, especially if you have large collections of documents.
4. **Set Up Shared Folders**: Create shared folders with team members for collaborative work. This simplifies file sharing and ensures that everyone has the latest version.
5. **Use the OneDrive App**: Download the OneDrive mobile app for easy access to files on your phone or tablet.

Frequently Asked Questions (FAQ)

Here are answers to the most common questions OneDrive beginners may have:

1. How do I upload files to OneDrive?

- You can upload files to OneDrive by dragging and dropping them into the OneDrive folder on your computer, or by using the "Upload" button in the OneDrive web app. Files can also be automatically uploaded from your phone using the OneDrive app.

2. How do I share files with others in OneDrive?

- To share a file or folder, right-click on the item and select the "Share" option. You can choose to send a link to others or send the file directly via email. You can also set permissions to allow others to view or edit the file.

3. What should I do if I reach my storage limit on OneDrive?

- If you reach your storage limit, you can upgrade to a larger storage plan or clean up unnecessary files by moving them to your computer or deleting them. Consider using a OneDrive plan with more storage if you need additional space.

4. How can I restore a deleted file from OneDrive?

- If you accidentally delete a file, check the OneDrive Recycle Bin. Files will stay there for a limited time (usually 30 days) before being permanently deleted. You can restore files from the Recycle Bin by selecting them and clicking "Restore."

5. Can I access OneDrive files offline?

- Yes, you can use the OneDrive app to download files for offline use on your device. Once the files are synced to your device, you can access them without an internet connection.

6. What are the benefits of using OneDrive for Business?

- OneDrive for Business offers enhanced security features, integration with SharePoint and Microsoft Teams, and greater control over file permissions and collaboration. It is specifically designed for business environments where file sharing and collaboration are essential.

7. How do I prevent others from viewing my shared files?

- When sharing files, you can set permissions that limit access. You can choose whether others can only view the file or if they can also edit it. Additionally, you can apply password protection and expiration dates to shared links.

8. What is the best way to back up my files with OneDrive?

- To back up your files, simply store them in your OneDrive folder. You can set up automatic syncing to ensure that files are continuously backed up. You can also manually upload specific folders or files you want to back up.

9. How do I sync files between OneDrive and my computer?

- Install the OneDrive desktop app and sign in with your Microsoft account. Once set up, files in your OneDrive folder will automatically sync with the cloud, and you can access them from any device.

10. Is OneDrive secure?

- Yes, OneDrive uses encryption to protect your files both in transit and at rest. It also offers security features like two-factor authentication to safeguard your account and data.

Index